Lampshades for Mothmen

Poems by Frederick Chamberlain

Lampshades for Mothmen
Copyright 2025© Frederick Chamberlain
Cover and interior illustrations- William Jackson

All rights reserved. Blue Jade Press, LLC retains the right to reprint this book. Permission to reprint poems from this collection must be obtained by the author.

ISBN- 978-1-961043-10-7

Published by:

Blue Jade Press, LLC

Blue Jade Press, LLC
Vineland, NJ 08360
www.bluejadepress.com

This book is dedicated to everyone that I have had the pleasure of meeting in my life.

And to:
My twin brother Steve,
for always being a beautiful man,
Jenna, the rose behind the inferno
Erica, my love, the Staten Island mermaid
Andrew duck, Raymond man, and Jason Schwartz for being amazing friends
Samantha Preston my beloved student who helped me share my art with the world
Lindsey, Uncle Harry and Melinda
My uncle Shawn who has always been a role model
My father who taught me so much
Richard and Marie Schwartz for always being there and for their undeserved kindness

and to my son, Bryan for who I hold all the love I can ever muster

"Sometimes you will never know the value of a moment, until it becomes a memory."

-Dr Seuss

Table of Contents

Daily Sacrifices	1
Aluminum Winter	2
Love's Journey	3
In My Dreams	4
There is no Ra Here	5
What is a Mothman, but Darkness?	6
The Yellow Eyes Never Lie	7
Love Turned into Hate	8
Aquatic Romance	9
Whom Do I Owe?	11
In My Haste to Evolve	12
Silence is Golden	13
Take Flight	14
Sartré's Alarm Clock	15
Buckets of Bullshit	16
Everything is not Okay	17
Crystal Balls Love Wallets	18
Snake in a Garden	19
A Man in Crimson Attire	20
The Closing of the Act	21
Blurred Lines	22
Barren Gaia	23
Calendar Days	24
Melancholy in Carcosa	25
What is Perfection?	26
Ebb & Flow	27
XOXO	28
Serving Two Masters	29
Give Me Chills, Blood Soaked Trojan Hills	30
Mothman	31
.45	32
Praise the Sun	33
Efreet's Crucible	34

Lobotomy	35
The Man in Yellow	36
The Night Man	37
Goodbye	38
Who Knew it was so Tidy in Here	39
Pandemonium without a Handbasket	40
Retired Clown	41
Simply Clay	42
Just Stardust	43
Balance	44
Hero of November	45
High on Oxytocin	47
Alley Cat	48
Subservience to the Moon	49
Snip Snip	50
The Moment She Vanished	51
Clinging	52
God Killer	53
Angel of Despair	54
Eight of Swords	55
Lampshades for Mothmen	56
Slave Ships	57
Lies of Face	58
Origin of Everything	59
Behind the Inferno	60
Despised by Gaia	61
On the Fence	62
Take it ALL	63
Lunar Body	64
Nothingness	65
Ignorance	66
Existential Dilemma	67
At the Apex	68
Songbirds	69
Neutral	70

Whimsical Defiance	71
Never Horizontal	72
Who is What They Say They Are?	73
Soul Balance	74
Capitol Hill	75
Smoking Kills	76
Love Lost	77
Decisions of Choice	78
Unchained	79
Don't Wait for Me	80
Do as Your Told	82
Who is Above Eternity	83
Funeral Pyre	84
Destined For More	85
Tripping Face Geometric Shape	86
Metallic Winter	88
Arggggggg	89
Eleanor	90
Fear the Reaper	91
Lies	92
The Clown with Makeup On	93
Head Organs	94
Man in the Mirror	95
Luminous Luminary	96
Lothric	97
Ann	98
Dancing in Circles	99
Melancholy Mornings	100
Twilight in Carcosa	102
The Web	103
Choices	104
Beautiful Memories	105
The Fiery Rose	106

Daily Sacrifices

I drew blood, for fool's gold
What is the sacrifice for hot showers?
What do you endure daily
just to sleep in gypsum?
Do you constantly right-hand swipe
cupid's game?
Theatrics are the worst
shop politics it's called
I would be content in an inyooət tent

I'm firmly rooted
for Gaia's meaning is to end
book of the damned, inked in pen
embracing the nocturne
welcoming sleep
drifting, like rings on a tree
expanding to ouroboros

Aluminum Winter

Tie-dyed, December,
drenched in metallic paint
critical mass'ed, field portabella's
seen the geometric shapes
180°demon eye (-Ides) landscape
The sleet came down like hammers
here in aluminum winter
sprinkled with silver
minutes could have stood still
if not for the shrew

It's in an observation blink
satiated fraction of time
the complete absurdity of it all
I remember gazing through glass
of a lady who lost a husband

Love's Journey

Climbing August mountains,
avoiding baleful storms
I only ever wanted to feel your breadth
hand and hand at the apex

I often stumbled, hands bled
mind numbs from exquisite impediment

Child of Nephilim so beautiful
eclipsing obscuring distress
a cacophony of gales

The summit is never near
no matter how hard I try
a mouse does not escape the bucket

In My Dreams

I hurtled into the blackest depths
and saw the giant eye of apocrypha

Ancient traveling through rivers out of time
terror is what my puny mind could conceive
for the eye eclipsed me, likened to an atom
approaching the sun

Frustration leads me to conclusions
Why have I been chosen?
the unraveling is the worst part
accepting it for what it is
a devourer devoid of human reasoning

I can't escape its gaze
nor can I run from its sight
I claw at my eyes begging to be released
death would seem welcoming
like a pie on a windowsill

I know it sees me, how can it not
How do you beg for mercy
against a creature like this?

There is no Ra Here

On ashen beaches
washed up on obsidian shores
there is no Ra here, only Nox
cloudless skies adorned with gems
precious things amongst the many

Few in number reach the climax
begging for warmth
the tardigrade is afraid to enter
for barren is the ass of Gaia

So very tired, I am
clinging to an inevitable end
yet I haven't clasped hands
nor have I begged
nor have I engaged
in treacherous thoughts

I will not be circumvented
you can't outwit the sphinx
or the three sisters

What is a Mothman, but Darkness?

I've given in to despair
I've fought too long and given in
to my most cumbersome tirades

What is a man, but darkness
ascension has granted me some leniency
granted an audience with old gods
the flesh bounds me in a prison
screaming and clawing till cranial flesh scraps

Underestimating the fabric of the celestials
I have— a dwarf star in its infancy
doesn't know its own destiny

I have been a shit person, bound by idiot chains
inescapable, crude designs made to torture
I often wonder why
the girl chose the bird as a means to escape

My guess is to fly away
from the hell-scape of rape
but can a little warble survive
the brutal world where there are no rules
no trial for the raven as it desecrates the corpse

The Yellow Eyes Never Lie

Does your heart wax and wane
is it as light as a feather?
I can't remember who it was
that drove me to madness

All I can recall was the song
that crashed upon the shore

To have never felt embraces in Carcosa
reeling from the den
sulfur brings vision
sometimes pleasant

Love Turned into Hate

A landslide of lies painted gold
a fever dream of unknowns
Midas was cursed so they say

Disappointment being an under-statement
completely losing all stocks invested
just a waste of fractal minutes
in accordance with father time
Insignificant cur!

If I could tar and feather I would
exiled to Australia
Love turned into hate
a story as old as time
I should have known better
for the moth doesn't reproduce
with the caterpillar

Aquatic Romance

The days are long
and the night's stamina draining
desperately trying
to bring you to squirter town
like striking oil
a prospector finding veins

I give it my all, 110%
just trying my damndest
for aquatic-romances

I would walk into a hail of submachine guns
just to lock eyes with you

Whom Do I Owe?

I used to enjoy my company
now I loathe it
maybe it's the realization
that I am in fact human garbage

The utter contempt I have for myself
and humanity as a whole, I digress...

The pendulum, you see, swings
I will get paid filthy human money
to buy filthy human goods and services
and hopefully by the grace of the Yellow eye
I will feel chemicals

Existing while better men
receive denarii's for Charon
to tread the line between glass fringes
upon escaping absurdity itself
am I not just an abused whore by definition
Who do I owe whore tithing money?

In My Haste to Evolve

So easily, I want to flip the board
suffocate the human chords
what is a moth to a flame
but another casualty
Can Gaia be saved?

Some things can't be reversed
forked tongues or murder
enlightened men will be outcasts
and they will scream aloud

"Why have you forsaken me?"

In my haste to evolve
I left remnants of my humanity
locked in a vault of memories
as I age Pandora's box always unlocks
to remind me of pain's glory
Can a God suffer
and if he can't lament
is he truly superior?

Silence is Golden

Stolen memories of untamed malevolence
haunt the id
trying to dictate to morons
whose very lives have helped no one

Their pitiful existence matters nil
at the zero hour, they'll be those that cower
hopefully recounting the idiocracy
that is their lives

They tell me not to blur the lines
hate being intolerant to their selfish bellies
in which they gorge the crowds
bullshit by the bucket-full

If I had to pick a side, it would be that of
Wyrmwood the Destroyer

I envy the blind deaf and dumb
for they don't have to listen to self-righteousness
drool from the lips of the closed minded
positioning themselves in trenches
of gnashing teeth

Take Flight

Upon escaping your temporal prison
you will metamorphose
into a stunning nebula
effulgent with pure starlight
a culmination of your inherent splendor

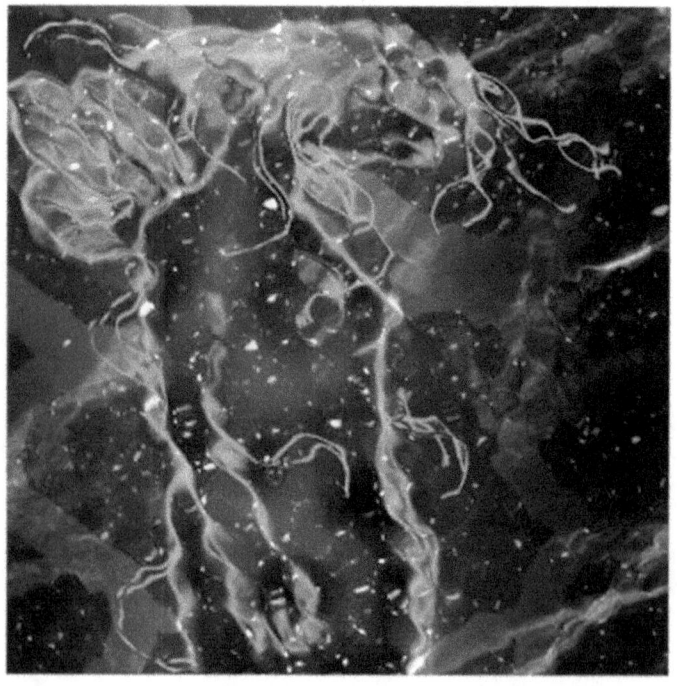

Sartré's Alarm Clock

Suitable emotions - an easy way
for us to navigate the uncomfortable

Does the woodpecker believe that it is the best
pecker of wood?

I've tried to mislead myself
of course it's a lot harder than it sounds
to no avail

Can snails sin?

Did the dinosaurs regard their bio-claw prints by
holding Pangea town meetings?

I don't understand the world around me
it's silly, imaginative, delusional
another man's dreamland

My gripe, you could say
would be with time
insignificant as lifespan

Wake up to the alarm clock
and before you even put on socks
you lie to yourself that you matter
or anything you do matters

We start our days dishonest

Buckets of Bullshit

I've tried to reason with walls
gums flap nonessential bullshit

Conversation demands chess clock moves
can't even have time to think
in a race with who can blab the loudest

I'd rather vow silence
than have to explain things to adult lemmings

Those who disregard their past
and forget how they got there infuriates me
it's all fine and dandy
as long as it's not your castle crashing

I've not only loved more than I should
but I've cared too much;
I fear being alone with the thoughts
a child's fear
"That guy can't get along with anybody"

Maybe I'm to blame?
I've stretched myself to my tensile limit
just wanted to be loved
just to be disrespected, ignored, unwanted

A Stockholm prisoner with a "Kick me" sign
you could give up the keys to El Dorado
and not even get a thank you

Everything is not Okay

When tragedy struck the chord
reverberating feelings of unease
disheveled in appearance

Lurking behind a white veil
comfortable in auspicious gains
traveling barefoot through knives
keeping my mind preoccupied and unencumbered
giving the piece of mind its compensation

If the mind is a dune field
then it all started with a grain
I saw the rose behind the flames
and my faculties malfunctioned

It is in these moments
ambrosia tastes like shit
and cold water drank
feels like sandpaper

Crystal Balls Love Wallets

The chains rattle songs of madness
a brain incapable of reason

As reality melts,
so does the mirror man
clutching so hard
the tendons snap

Should I slide idly by
as the stoked fire rages forth
an inferno that has consumed all consumables
lingering onwards on hate alone
shunned, mocked, disrespected
burning on DETERMINATION

YOU CAN'T HAVE MY NICKELS FOR I
NEED TO PAY THE FERRYMAN

Destined death they call it
crystal balls love wallets

Snake in a Garden

Gold rivets stitched on alabaster
truly stunning to behold

For a snake slithers
with disagreeing eyes
maligned for chaos
Could it be the abyss that made you
hate corporeal creations?

For I am just as confused as you are
Why then does man seek the *eyes* of March?

The chaos in those yellow eyes only
to the observant can one truly understand

I choose nothing
for nothingness is truly poetical
save your breath
Melpomene and Thalia
for the last performance

A Man in Crimson Attire

How can every single one of you go on
the thin man plots, to fill plots
the unseen degree of 33
makes you vomit
truly dark times is that why
he traveled to Drangleic?
undeserving under servants
playing chess in 4D

The Closing of the Act

Have you ever stumbled?
Have you ever chosen the closing of the act
over brain emotions?

May the applause be my only supplication
thunderous echoes the reason of my-being

CRICKETS VIBRATING AT THE
ONE MAN SHOW

May I have this dance monsieur?
the world could be ripped asunder
as long as I have you, monsieur

Blurred Lines

To advance for science sake
I forsake humanity
for dead flesh shall reanimate

My life's obsession, my deterministic
unbreakable vow to spit in the face of GOD...
yet, they called me the monster

Barren Gaia

Lost your connection to Gaia
through rubber soles
destined for dystopia
an asphalt farmer
tilling her bare

Calendar Days

As the calendar ends
so does belief
in all things considered
leaves one often-bewildered
casting lots to define choice

I am an animal's rage
left caged for betterment
things left for better men
spiraling through madness
with opaque eyes
comfy in all things residual
degradation grants an end
to nirvana's wheel

Melancholy in Carcosa

On the beach
I sat unencumbered
by the why of it all
madness takes hold very gently
it's never abusive

Once you've seen the eye on the spire
happiness is as foreign
as breathing underwater

In desperate need
to open the numerous neuron pathways
you might find specks of joy

Awareness breeds suspicion
like a back alley London meat pie

What is Perfection?

I don't live in a perpendicular palace
I can't live with your
interpretation of flawlessness
I won't go idly trotting into shit pastures
I will continue to be,
just until the zero hour
come bring your tired to the Land of Oz
Sit them on pedals
strip them of bi-pedals
If thought was a person... would it look like you?

Ebb & Flow

The tides sing a melody through
the ebb and flow of the waves
swimming ever deeper
its melodic voice drags you under

Never did I wander unto great fortune
for its shine offers only the brave comfort
stagnating death putrid in its appearance
looms like an enviable king

If death had a face it would be beautiful
adorned with jewels
I'll begin to sink into unending miserable misery
if there's no plan or purpose
how can chess pieces move

I envy the tribes of the Amazon
I feel that they are not existentialists
the obligation I have for this world doesn't exist

XOXO

You're the greatest thing since Betty White
you sparkle with luminescence

You are ambrosia
a face like vineyard wine
to sleep next to you is divine
to wake with you is equivalent
to a snail becoming a CEO
of a silicon valley start-up

You brighten up my life
by your mere existence
by just existing like an autumn leave
you vex me, challenge me
leave me on the edge of my seat in anticipation

I would be honored to be with you
and to share the moments with you
XOXO

Serving Two Masters

I received a letter from the estuary
where the great rivers converged
the note is not important
it's existence is likened to an alarm clock
that starts one's day

The reasons behind the veil of written word
are not interesting in the slightest
it reads like a yawn
how can one interpret Prometheus
while entreating Efreet's feather in the cap
it answered nothing
but added questions about a cruel abacus
it no longer matters to me what you write

Give Me Chills, Blood Soaked Trojan Hills

The love I have for you
Midas himself would envy its power
driven by smittens kisses

The Trevi fountain is beauty incarnate
as if Aphrodite herself used transmogrify
if I could only capture such bliss
as a junkie takes in their first hit....

I could never fully explain in words
the magnificence of caring about someone
to literally pour every ounce of yourself
to even laying down one's life

The very notion going against your own instincts
give me chills blood soaked Trojan hills

Mothman

My haunted expressions tell a story
a tale of excessive abuse

No longer am I still here
I've begun my transformation
into what I do not know
for the moth doesn't mingle
with the caterpillar

Feeling tired can't control the urge
to dissolve into nothingness

.45

Never could have imagined it
destined death with Lucille

Never in a million years would I have thought
that pretty Lucille would have taken me out

You were my favorite companion
always in close proximity

Made papa super proud, 30 rounds
I am glad it was you after all

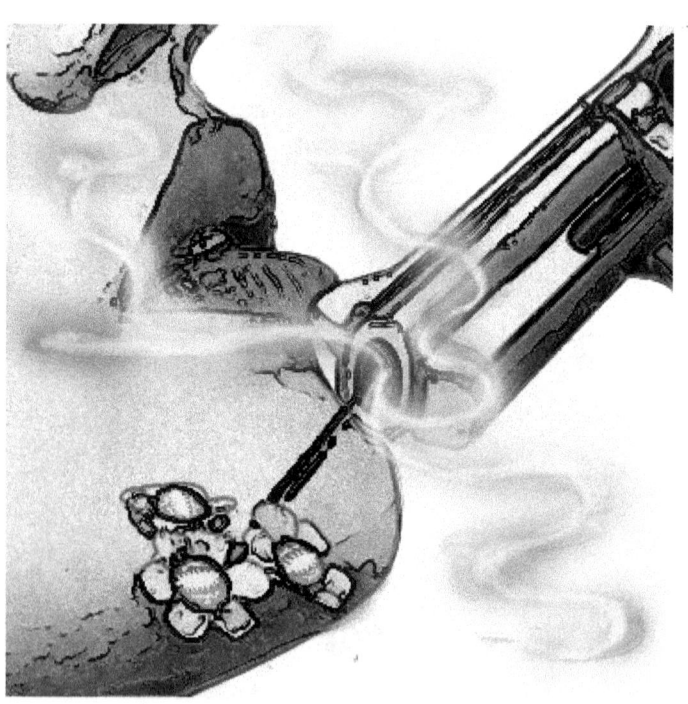

Praise the Sun

Heaven's host golden eye of Ra
piercing, blinding through midmorning's dew
don't blink, embrace his warmth
glory incarnate the one above all

I forgive you for turnt blue neon fluorescence
I applaud your efforts and your splendor
making giants dance

"Who am I but an insignificant cur compared to your divinity, sir?"

Efreet's Crucible

I was born in fire
a true aspect of Efreet's crucible
a rage so burning bright
searing beneath my flesh
I would rouse the ancient one
with the aura of my anger

Frustration leads me down paths
that converge unto pain
then forks into madness
I shudder to aforementioned
the kindling of a lucky strike
the shame of two mortals

My true and only sin on Gaia is
that I would sever
the electrical connection
to the universe
and awaken chaos immortal

Lobotomy

Opened the gloam door
felt the sudden shock
of being unable to receive oxygen
a suffocating nauseum

Opening my forehead iris
was the worst thing
I could have done
ignorance is truly bliss
for the spoon never exists to begin with

I would gladly accept Gehenna's flame
I stubbornly flip the board on the game

The Man in Yellow

During a festival
a man pulled me aside
and asked me
if I knew the man in yellow
I assured him I had not

He is a man of madness
a king of the absurd
the ego, the ID
and the primordial

The Night Man

The night man beckons
crowns the mad monk in yellow
you want enlightenment
until you don't
you find understanding
just to go reeling into darkness infinite
scraping flesh from cranial bone
they say be weary of your djinn request
the books in Alexandria burnt to cinders
man was never meant to cave paint
or to find wisdom in triangles

Goodbye

Dismayed over thoughts
a cascade of memories
Did you have to dance with death?
an abused lover that loved
to waltz with nothingness
just to feel nothing; you lost everything
as blood siphoned into the chamber

Did you think of me?
Was it worth it?

Without batting an eye
you went into eternal night
my sorrow is over your lack of strength
to fight wrestle with your demons
and battle for life!
if it were easy
no one would have evolved

My beloved, I hope the maggots
didn't eat your soul
I hope it's over
and your consciousness hasn't ascended

Who Knew it was so Tidy in Here

Through my dreams
I saw the grand inquisitor
legions upon legions of eyes
the true horror was the organization
that was kept tidy
obsessive-compulsive dark God's
it's enough to make you laugh

In all my cosmic thought provoking stratagem
nothing could ever prepare
me for what I beheld
in my dream I began to sing a lullaby
I could not begin to tell you why
be it shock, fear
or a complete meltdown of my psyche
I began to recite lyrics I never knew
harmonious to a melody
I couldn't have imagine

Pandemonium Without a Handbasket

Hark!
Who goes through pandemonium
without a handbasket
through the looking glass
too much glucose for my absinthe

Have you ever trembled so hard
with a clenched fist
that you drew life's essence

Tranquility in excess leads to extinction
I don't want to live
within a chamber of indulgence
nothingness awaits me
like a wayward lover

Retired Clown

Stopped performing
retired my nose
can no longer hold back thoughts
a torrent of ideas
entertain the masses
I cannot

Evolved man has no place in Eden
with all the strength and energy I can muster
I must demolish my former being

"For the caterpillar has no say in the matter?"
asked Alice to the Hatter

Simply Clay

Twisted guile
play the symbol monkey
Terra's clay
begging for the star
In my desperation
I clung to Charon's cloak
the summation of life is that it ends
am I no better than a tree?
IS immortality really simplistic
my complexities betray me

Just Stardust

In the end just stardust
even 4th planets rust
no need for sorry
bad things happen
to good people every day
the universe takes no prisoners

Balance

Forged in the crucible
when laziness and complacency
siege lesser creatures

I rise like Jörmungandr
I have truly evolved past humanity
I am the savior of a celebratory peace meal
I piss golden sparkling excellence

What motivates you I wonder
thoughts in tidal waves

Bow down, to the hero of November
prostrate before me
like a human jellybean
causality holds me no longer
your lives are dust
for what is a man's life
compared to a turtle or a tree

You're asking the wrong *preguntas*

Hero of November

I was lost for so long
dying of a thirst
I could never satiate or understand
nothingness calls to me
like a prison break
I've continued to the last pages of the book
I've become repetition
a bead on the abacus
lamenting over reality
as a means to cope
be delicate in what you wish for
the Divine tree wept
for it had to watch
as everything dies

Who am I to deny the queen of the museum?

High on Oxytocin

Two weirdos high on oxytocin
she made my heart sing
never have I ever
she was the queen
of the looking glass
regal in all things
sparkles love of my life
a prisoner on a wayward planet
in a wayward time consuming dream
words could never express my gratitude
for saving me
not even knowing
I was lost to begin with

Alley Cat

In my earnest I may have acquired
a cat so beautifully broken
created by the chaos
of primordial creation

Here kitty kitty
come to my lap and purr
heed the sirens call
and be made jelly in my hands

Shall I give her a name my bi-pedal pet?

Subservience to the Moon

Thirsty grass sips on dew
the tides themselves
subservient to the moon
I have seen the darkest part
of the human soul
I gave you discomfort
in the form of a flower petal
I spoon-fed you
what you wanted to hear
and told myself lies

Snip Snip

There once was a lobster so proud and free
he snipped and snapped most joyfully
his life was not a fight for paper
it was existence on existence's terms

Laughter and glee
is all this crustacean has ever known
no one instructs my vision
I am free to snap my claws
which beats the alternative
of not snip snapping

The Moment She Vanished

The moment she vanished
it became apparent still I clung
reassured by your gnashing tongue, oh!
oh, bitter one can be
when the door slams shut
What could I do?

Just a tiny, insignificant speck in the cosmos
do I try to define destiny with my mind
I believe not

Ps. I hold solace in the comfort that in your bloodlust, you willingly destroyed my world... you, in your incredible haste, forgot the fact like the Phoenix, I thrive in the ashes.

Clinging

Begin Anu end Tathamet,
just you and the spin of the die
when thine globe withers
and meets a forever winter

Some will claim Jacob's ladder
with veiny heart in hand
light as a feather
if only we had the brightest stars
maybe tragedy would not befall us all
if I could, I would pluck
the very eyes from Nostradamus

God Killer

If you had the strength of will
to forge a god-slaying weapon
would you use it?

Would you herald death
and throw him into Gehenna?

Even with the fabric of reality at stake
would you still use it?

Would you smile like Sisyphus
or laugh with Prometheus?

Angel of Despair

Angel of despair
let me fall
let me fall
release me from your mighty arms
let me descend into
unfathomable
miserable
misery
no need to fix your gaze
my peace isn't your purpose
my wants are not your concern

Eight of Swords

Plucked the eight of swords
myself being my worst villainous enemy
have you ever strangled yourself
pressed so hard and left thumb marks
stagnation unmotivated
is the greatest student
to ever live
no teacher has assigned the task
so I'll wait for instructions
What to do about my restraints?
Best to leave that to better-men-t, lobotomy?

Lampshades for Mothmen

Roaming the earth, undiagnosed
no filter, aww, would you
like beautiful lies instead
I'm insignificant, you're insignificant
to put it into perspective
a bee is more significant

Telling no falsehoods, humans want honesty
but can't handle the logical facts
living in truth surrounds you in darkness
awareness brings back your light
and when you're humble and know your place
your candle burns bright

Your inner illumination fights off the night
chases the clouds for three mother moonlight
you read my thoughts but are you even listening
twenty-five of the greatest among you
isn't worth one bee

Slave Ships

Consciousness eclipsed by brigadier ships
closing in then, blink
waves so loud, piercing howls
chains rattle underfoot
the stench of panic and piss pervaded my nostrils
I'll die here better to die to Davy Jones
than be treated like property

Lies of Face

I am tired of forced rhetoric
tired of the dance
tired of the fake pleasantries
I hate you all,
and I would like you to know
the gift of existence
is not a present for all
time and time again
I searched for the scales to balance
only to find Ammut's ravenous hunger

Origin of Everything

I pushed so hard
harder than I ever should
I gradually became
what I feared the most
even as the thorns ripped
my skin from bone
I pushed

Even when I was swallowed
by the bramble
I pushed harder still
as the blood splattered
it was getting hard to breathe
I realized the rose departed

With my final breath, I curse the very beginning
the origin of everything that was, and will ever be

Behind the Inferno

It came to be, when the raven screamed
hollow dreams of clandestine scenes
to the 70's to notice, to the 80's to care
life is funny but never fair
I paid a maiden to heal my ribcage organ
she could never be the desert rose
behind the inferno
I should shudder
at the aforementioned sentence
but it all has fallen apart

Despised by Gaia

Vessels of Adam
languid husks
despised by Gaia
blighted legacy
not a decent one
among you
what a beautiful allegory
wouldn't you agree
moral of the story...
plant a fucking tree

On the Fence

Walking through the door of mistrust
duality they call it
if and when I trust a person
I am left disheartened and dismayed
equality thru Cartesian dualism
the classic tale of broken glass
why would you open the act one on the play
if you were just going to take it all away
devastated is truly an understatement
with complete understanding
you preordained, my torture stake

Take it ALL

Take all that makes me, me
Take it all!
All that I was, all that I will ever be
Take my very identity
Take my thoughts, my dreams, my aspirations
Take it all!
I give it freely of my own volition
Take my sadness take my pain
take my hardships
Take it ALL!!!!!
MY NOUNS
MY ADJECTIVES
MY VOICE
MY BLOOD
TISSUE,
ORGANS

Lunar Body

Stand alone on the lunar body
dance and sway to your own orbit
do not be eclipsed by dwarfs of fire
stand-alone lunar body

Nothingness

From vermillion hills
to urban balconies
I wander aimlessly
I took offense through
the gate of ambivalence
I stripped down my mind
to just breathing
no need to think
while at the zenith of the abyss

What awaits lurking in everlasting darkness?
Something ancient beyond time?

Ignorance

I've become cold and calculating
frantically screaming at no one
I sure as hell didn't get myself here
could have never gotten here by myself
that will be the day listening
to a fragile bi-pedal animal
that doesn't command power over
its own dwarf star
ignorance is truly bliss

Existential Dilemma

The prisons that bind our minds
inescapable by design
tragedy begins anew like spring flowers
Carpe diem
funny how the little things add
and compound like a micro transaction
calculated on an abacus made of filth and bile

At the Apex

Tears I shed from atop high
as I stood bewildered
at the apex of creation

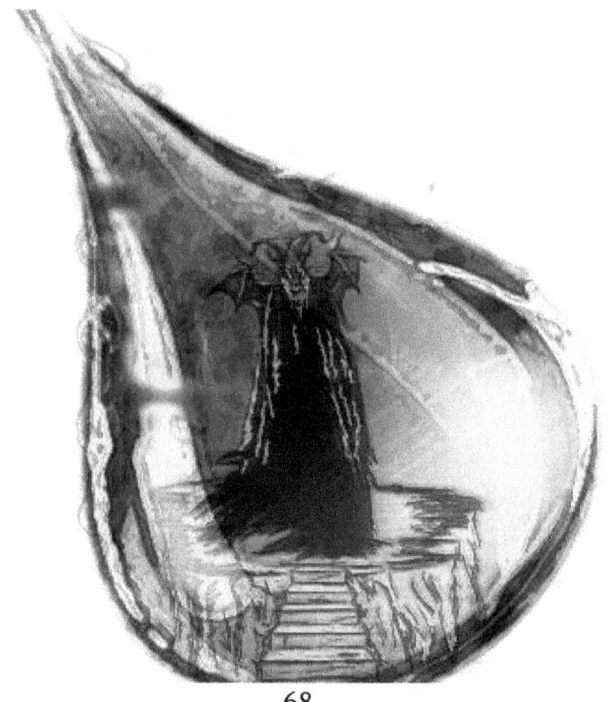

Songbirds

Hey,
Have you made the songbirds late?
They are never late
Sometimes early but never late
Mark the date when you made the songbirds late
Deliver unto me your ancient morning's decree!
Why are they not here?
Why do I not hear them?
A hole in my heart shattered to pieces
Crystalline organ meat

Neutral

In a perpetual dream state
as my mind drifts
Obliteration Declarations
because I occupy space
does not give me the right
to hinder another's progress
Regress?
Is neutrality truly the answer?

Whimsical Defiance

Forging ahead, boring regrets
stretching my legs
comfort I once sought-after
no longer reliant whimsical defiance
Can I give up now?
I've fulfilled my end of the bargain
I've filled your blood coffers to the brim
ambivalence has taken roots
stuck in a nightmarish hell-scape
of fraudulent visages

Never Horizontal

Not a care did I have
not at that particular moment
slice vertical they said

Who is What They Say They Are?

When Tartarus erupts and hell spills forth
will you run towards the fire?
Have you made peace with the Reaper?
How many would throw children
into a wood-chipper, to save themselves?
When Wyrmwood descends
will you cower like a subterranean rodent?
Or will you welcome death
on death's terms smiling?

Soul Balance

Who knows?
stripped thine flesh from bone
blood and sinew put on a scale
10 pence insignificant
my species is
lost its stardust

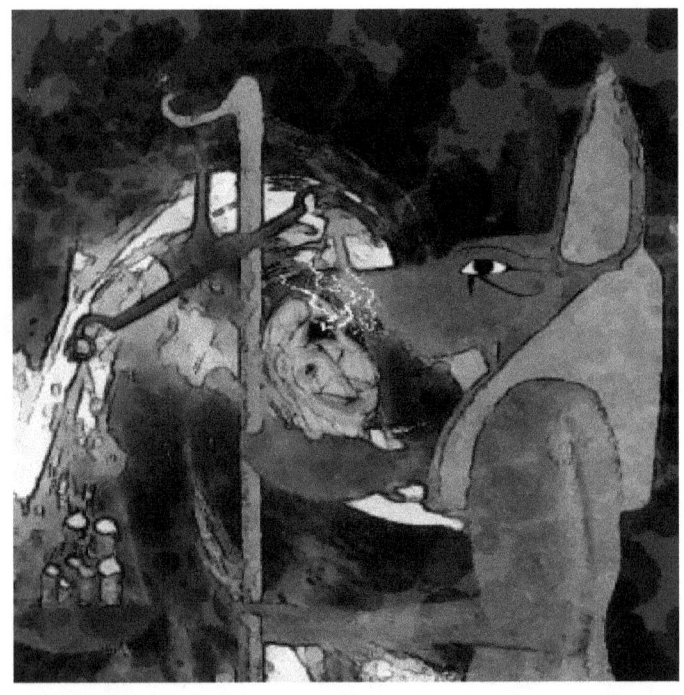

Capitol Hill

Over there on Capitol Hill
I made an odd gesture
I pulled my trousers down
and started propelling Sir Richard

Smoking Kills

Uhmm... As I scream out
with agonizing distress
bound by a feeble mind
for only an ogre
would force me against my will
to habitually ingest toxins
chemicals, cancer, tar

Only a truly sadistic
psychologically impaired mind
would allow such suffrage
as I slowly die
and suffer immensely
here imprisoned
in a cage of bone

Love Lost

I can't fill the void, I hate you
but I don't want you to be destroyed
overwhelming guilt drags
feeble minds to obsidian prisons
I once beheld a desert rose in full bloom
if I could erase time itself, I would
if I could go back to that particular inferno
to see the flowers through
the flames just once more
just the incessant need and want to clog
the hole in my pump organ
I would retrieve the very head of
Mr. Iscariot from the ninth circle of hell

Decisions of Choice

The ebb and flow of my desires
tranquil on its surface, chaotic at its core
obligated to choose neutrality, to gaze
eyes behold to seas of gray area
I only speak the truth do you not get it?
My mind can change directions, in mere seconds!
I could abhor murder, and kill you barehanded

See where the conflict arises
See why I hold such contempt for men-of-flesh

Unchained

Alone and happy once more
the tasks are done
the daily repetitive
migraine inducing
eye twitching
mandates accomplished
I am now free from human bonds
what seemed like inescapable chains
become dust as I drift towards
evolutionary God-hood
at the behest of my alarm clock
I will have to give up my divinity
for the mornings bring obligation
damn you moral compass

Don't Wait for Me

Don't wait for me
I am not coming back
I have burnt down the bridge
that connected us

All I have taken is memories
cherished by me, forever
being abandoned at birth
makes me really good
at saying goodbye
your death only leads
to my rebirth
essence transfer perhaps

As I soared towards the sun, the wax began to run.

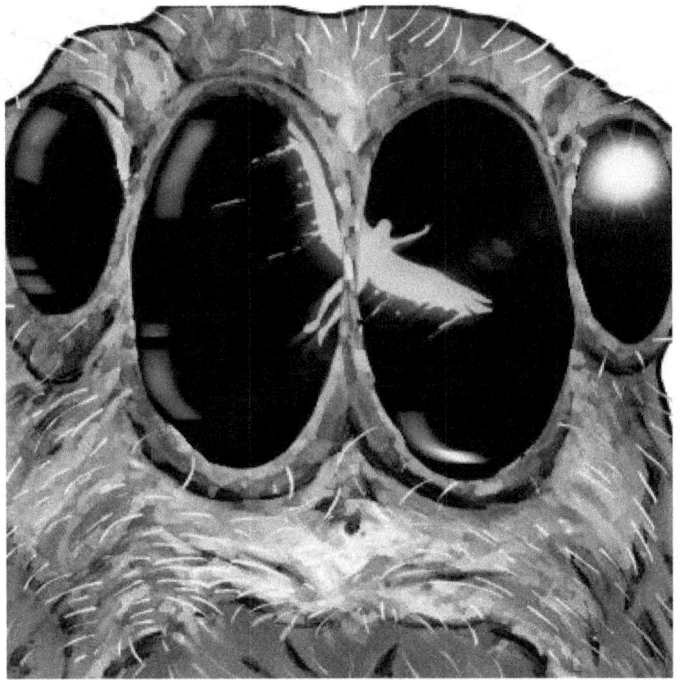

Do as Your Told

Hypocrisy is a funny thing
vying for thrones of a kingdom of bones
a moral compass with no direction
on the proverbial fence
never to set foot on land human stalactites
scenarios unfold and out of boldness
it's don't do what I do, do as you're told

Who is Above Eternity

Invoke enlightenment
and enter Shang-ri-la
for who is above eternity
now is the zero hour walk
and be branded by the misguided en masse
for who amongst man has traversed
the zenith of the Æthers
the lattice of all things
resides in mathematics
for it is immortality divine

Funeral Pyre

When I die, don't cry!
Rejoice in my forever sleep
my forever peace
burn me upon pillars of old gods
so I may get a glimpse of Shang-ri-la
betwixt roads led to hemlock groves
where reapers roam, names engraved on stone

Destined For More

What is man besides
a wretched pile of filth
no better than a parasite
given paradise chooses nuclear genocide
they ask me why are you a nihilist

I reply with sadness in my eyes
I want to skate on Saturn's rings
I want to not grow old in cryogenic sleep
nothingness appeals to me
more than fancy any things

Tripping Face Geometric Shape

Time and time went by
as quickly as the blink
the angles formed
shape the face of Metatron
so many eyes
with nowhere to hide
what could something so ancient
even ponder on
I could do nothing
for what am I
but a speck of dust?

I saw her beautiful sadness through the window;
she lost her love.

Metallic Winter

Metallic winter speckled silver delivers
me to my destination
I've eaten from the pustules
they are in New Jersey
as I sit here gazing upon metal Christmas
my heart did glee and it may have even bumped
oh how I've missed you Cheshire grin
so delighted I am staring at metallic winter

Argggggg

I have an anger inside me
deep within me
it swells and manifests
it is an ugly thing
an anger so bitter and wretched
old Catholicism would bind me
they would say that a demon is inside me
if ever I was so complacent
as to unlock this cage of rage
the recipient of this rabid dog
would indeed be frightened
his instincts heightened

Eleanor

Went soul searching
down the bayou
looking for the crossroads
to make a deposit
bought a little lady at the market
named her Eleanor
left everything I ever was
back in the city of brotherly love
at the devil's betwixt roads
I made a bargain

"You there marry me and Eleanor"
let her voice vibrate, let it be vibrant

Fear the Reaper

Why so harshly judge me
stand on high above me
do you love the view
mathematics is divine
everything else is conjecture
so your berating lectures
fall on deaf drums
if what I do becomes conflict
then please drop the guillotine
for my persona does not fear the reaper

Lies

Facets engraved majestically upon
thine mantle made of flesh
embossed interlaced within
the fabric of perception
sands dissolve between
glass tick tocking

Within logical reasoning,
can a yellow stone
really be worth egregious sin?

The Clown with Makeup On

Such a trifling, loathsome endeavor
to put my mask on thine visage
and dance like the good ol' symbol monkey I am
I simply abhor such notions
but I'd likely admit
I'd gleefully enchant thyne guests
with the grace of a swan reeling
in their delightful cackles and caws
as if their admiration
could amuse me in the slightest

Head Organs

As I forge ahead on unstable footing
my mind reels from memories best forgotten

Is it too much to ask for leniency
from my own mind?

I digress, for the most beautiful of things
lives in the most harshest of environments
my temples have been ransacked by gluttonous
bi-pedal animals who can't even
govern blind footfalls

Man in the Mirror

LET THE GUILT MANIFEST!
LET THE NIGHTMARES OF YOUR
FALSEHOODS AND FAKE GUISE
SURROUND YOU!
SURRENDER TO YOUR OWN SHAME,
AND FALL UPON ASH CLOTH!
WRIGGLE AND WRITHE
AT THE THING IN THE MIRROR!

Luminous Luminary

She had a pallor of lavender always so cold
with a natural rouge mascara
I would gently marvel at her
stunning visual appearance
I could fill up the library of Alexandria
with her mood ring eyes
alas, for all her striking countenance
it was her essence I toss and turn at night
for luminance
brilliant, luminous, luminaries!
through the door you reach out for the light
switch frantically searching for the switch

Lothric

I care not for the tolling of the bells
or the gargoyles that bar my journey
driven only for my lust for power
I will journey on
an undead curse
go from here gentle whispers
caressing me in gentle kisses
make believe packed full of fantasy

Ann

Like sheets of satin
I've touched her
In the throes of passion
I've made her squishy
I gave up my mind and shattered my defenses
I handed my essence on silver dinnerware
like a pious man to God
I blindly stepped forward
I walked through brambles and thorns
Alas, to no avail
like a distressed pachyderm
I've fallen on knees
Oh, my dearest Ann
if only I was more dashing
I suppose...

Dancing in Circles

As the clock face reads one
I began to spin
faster than a whirlwind
such fun to turn 360°

Melancholy Mornings

Oh melancholy mornings,
why do you incessantly cause me grief?
There is no reason for your visit,
life's hard but it's not bad.
I guess you can tag along today
but only as a friend.
For I could never turn away a friend,
even a soul sucking toxic one.
Be warned though, my patience has its limits
you can't stay or take up residence here!

Has anyone seen
Mike or
Yanni or

Bill,
Ryan,
Andy,
Iris,
Ned?

Twilight in Carcosa

Twilight in Carcosa
the yellow sovereign idles away
time without remembrance
before Lake Cocytus formed any ice
or the master worker started the grand design
there on the beaches of Carcosa
a vortex of what was and what could never be
I stood here unraveling

The Web

Unbeknownst to the adult diptera
the more he struggled
the more entangled he became

Choices

Wayward and lost
my bearings are nihilistic
when given the choice
do I choose Charybdis over Scylla
the path less traveled by
did really make all the difference

Beautiful Memories

I have in the framework
of my cerebellum: an oasis
I fill only my most valuable things
within its boundaries
this treasure is not tangible
for it cannot be held

The Fiery Rose

I've made plenty of mistakes over and over
a hamster on a proverbial wheel
in a sea of seraphim, there was a rose
for I was given insight
and with insight breeds awareness
light in the darkness never feels threatening
its very presence is warm and inviting
a rose perhaps

Frederick Chamberlain is an average American living in the State of Pennsylvania. A welder by trade and a Mothman by night, Frederick started his writing journey after the end of a long-term relationship. His writing reflects an emotional tailspin that can take hold after the loss of a future planned. His poetry is a reflection of the madness that dwells within his brain, a man wanting to shed his mortal coil and become the midnight butterfly.

www.ingramcontent.com/pod-product-compliance
Lightning Source LLC
Chambersburg PA
CBHW071730090426
42738CB00011B/2436